WHITEBOARDS and WHATEVER

Fun Activities
for More Purpose,
Passion, Clarity and
a **Successful You!**
(Whiteboards Optional)

KIMBERLY KELSOE

ISBN 13: 978-1-946629-59-3

ISBN 10: 1-946629-59-6

ACKNOWLEDGMENT

I dedicate this book to my family and friends who have supported my passion for writing. I would like to thank my husband who has been patient with my many pursuits to find my passion. Also, I would like to thank my father who taught me how to write in my own style and showed me how to imagine and live my life without limits. Additionally, I want to thank all of the inspirational ladies in my life, especially my mom who has greatly contributed to my writing by being a great role model and sharing her many life lessons. My twin daughters,

Abigayle and Natalie, motivate me to always aspire for more. Natalie teaches me life lessons, including those of trust and kindness, and her interesting sense of humor impacts my life daily. Through her daily challenges, Abigayle has taught me that there is no limit to problem-solving opportunities! Finally, I would like to thank Michelle Prince and her team for making my writing dream a reality.

"Having a solid vision for your future is one of the most crucial steps in living a life of success and significance. In *Whiteboards and Whatever*, Kimberly Kelsoe shares easy to implement techniques and exercises that will help you gain more clarity and develop a game plan that will positively change your life. I highly recommend you read this little book with a big purpose!"

Michelle Prince
Best-Selling Author, Speaker, and Publisher
www.MichellePrince.com

"What a piece of inspiring work your book is! To say I enjoyed reading it will be a gross understatement. I must also tell you that it really helped me deal with some personal cobwebs that I have since erased and decluttered from my mind and life. This book will bring much-needed guidance to a lot of people in a simple and unpretentious manner. It is well written, easy to read and follow, and, most importantly, fun to read! The approach will make it appropriate for virtually all audiences. Thank you for doing this, and for sharing!"

Ali B. Mansaray
Director, STD/HIV and Viral Hepatitis Division
Bureau of Communicable Disease Prevention and Control (BCDPC)
South Carolina Department of Health and Environmental Control (SCDHEC)

"*Whiteboards and Whatever* takes the complicated topic of self-love, growth, and actualization, and makes it fun, engaging, and spirited. Kimberly Kelsoe has practical and uplifting ways of bringing readers with her to a new way of seeing what is possible with a little discipline, hope, and a plan! This is

a terrific primer for newbies or a perfect re-
fresher for anyone looking for new ways to
be healthy and happy."

Jennifer Hancock, LCSW
President and CEO
Volunteers of America Mid-States
Serving Kentucky, Tennessee, West Virginia,
and Clark and Floyd Counties in IN

"I believe you wrote something useful and
powerful. Your whiteboarding exercises can
be done by anyone who wants to better
themselves."

Fara Kral
Analyst 1, Rebates
California

"I am a person who does a lot of self-reflec-
tion, and I have ideas about what I would
like in the future. However, I have never really thought about putting those ideas into

action. The future is now, and the individual and group activities helped me to think more clearly about what actions to take. I worked on the individual activity on my own and then did it again with Kimberly as the moderator, and it was an amazing experience working with her. I am excited about my future and want to begin taking the steps toward an action plan. I couldn't have done this without Kimberly's activities and direction. Thank you!"

Terese Ghilarducci, MFT, PPS
Village High School Counselor
Pleasanton, California

"Realize your dreams with this book."

Regina Leung
Partner
Innovari Partners
California

"This book and the activities gave me the courage to get to know myself without limits."

Courtne Campbell-Key
Exceptional Student Education
Support Professional
Walton County School District, Florida

"I can't wait to hear about all the people this impacts!"

Kim Kelsoe
(the other Kim Kelsoe, sister-in-law)
Houston, Texas

"My experience with the whiteboarding activity was similar to therapy, in that I was able to recognize some things that I knew but never came to terms with internally. I found it cathartic because I had to acknowledge the things I was holding onto and realize the only way to grow professionally was to resolve the personal issues I was holding onto. In therapy, you can stay away from certain topics. During this activity, the whiteboarding topics can get brought up indirectly, so you have to acknowledge them."

Cathy Burton-Meza
Senior Manager
Audits & Compliance
San Bruno, California

"Kimberly is amazing! I left my whiteboarding experience with Kimberly feeling there are new possibilities for my future that I can make my reality. The whiteboarding experience is so empowering. It reminds you that you are worthy of your dreams and guides you to make them realized."

Julie Kettenring
Barnes & Noble
New Orleans, Louisiana

"The material generated an in-depth discussion with my son on the aspect of being aware to how others perceive you. The distinction you make about the others being people who care about you and not haters was important. I think young people (HS and college) should receive this in hopes that they make it an early habit/practice. I think most people would be flabbergasted. It is a motivational booklet worth reading and embracing!"

Kristina Hermach
Director
State Government Affairs
Washington

TABLE OF CONTENTS

CHAPTER 1

WHY THE WHITEBOARD

*"Happiness is not something
you postpone for the future;
it is something you design for the present."*
JIM ROHN

Would you like to know a secret? One of the most powerful tools you can use to find your purpose and get more clarity is readily available and can be found at your local office supply store. It is called a whiteboard. If you are not familiar with whiteboards, they are similar to a chalk-board, but with erasable markers.

Enter the conference room of any large corporation, and you will most likely find a whiteboard on the wall. Have you ever wondered why such a simple tool is so common in meeting rooms across the country?

It's simple. For many people, being able to write and draw out thoughts is one of the most effective tools for finding purpose and clarity.

> *Whiteboards can provide you a literal blank slate for visualizing your ideas, your inspirations, or the mind map of your life strategy.*

In this book, I will show you how you can successfully use this tool to develop the vision that will positively change your life, and you will have fun while doing it. You will also discover how using a whiteboard can help you further your own networking opportunities through group activities.

> ***A whiteboard can be the ultimate physical metaphor for your life.***

Your life can be like a blank slate, empty and ready for you to fill it in with whatever you please. The whiteboard is ready to receive your heart's desires, passions, and loves, as well as your heartbreaks, sorrows, and pains … and all in between. With a whiteboard, you have the power of a pen complemented by the convenience of an eraser.

In this book, I have included many practical ideas on how you can use a whiteboard as a productivity, problem-solving, and planning tool, starting today. Use the whiteboard to help you organize your thoughts, stretch your imagination, discover paths toward your full potential, and bring clarity and color to the blank spaces in your life. While I personally prefer using a whiteboard for the activities in this book, you can just as easily use a blank sheet of paper.

The key is to do the activities with whatever tool is most impactful and easiest to use over the long-term. I have heard that it takes 21 days for new habits to take root in us. If nothing else, just commit to doing the individual activity in Chapter 3 for 21 days to see what you can uncover for yourself and how you can develop new habits.

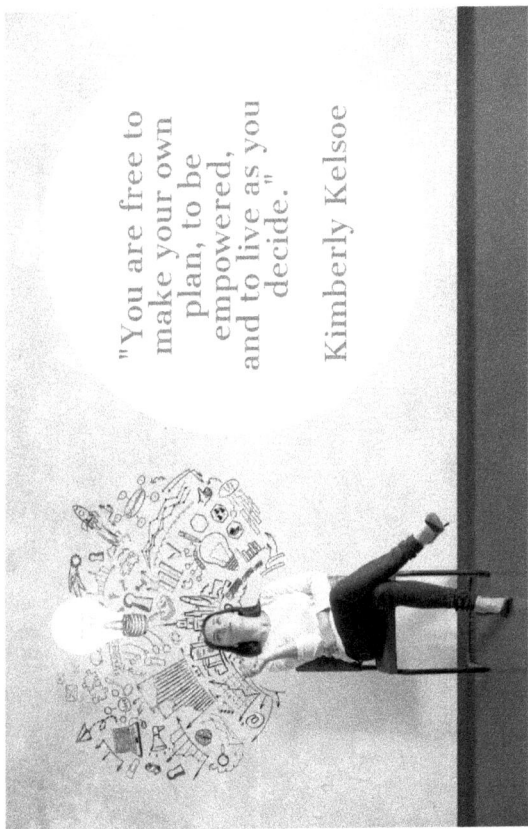

"You are free to make your own plan, to be empowered, and to live as you decide."

Kimberly Kelsoe

CHAPTER 2:

BEGIN PLANNING YOUR JOURNEY

"The journey of a thousand miles begins with a single step."

LAO TZU

Before you dive into the self-exploration and planning activities that I'll share with you, it's important to orient yourself towards positive thinking and a mindset free of limits. You hold the power to determine your future, so why not make it a good one!

> ***Don't worry about meeting
> any kind of expectations or
> reaching a certain level.***

As you work through some of the fun activities, remember that this is a journey, and don't put too much pressure on yourself. It is also a good reminder that our journey simply cannot be the same as another's journey, so you should celebrate, not compare.

It is most important for you to think of one key takeaway you can gain from the experience. That, in and of itself, is a huge WIN! You only need one good idea to take that next step. Complete the activities and you will make progress toward your dreams. It may be as simple as gaining more clarity in your life. Starting today, you can be on your new path of self-discovery, find your passion, and achieve more fulfillment in life.

Be EXCITED about your future!

No matter where you are in your life, you can make it even better. This is just the starting point of your potential. While your options are endless and your possibilities beyond imagination, focus on taking the first step. Too many times people get overwhelmed with the thought of a long and drawn-out journey.

"Who you are tomorrow begins with what you do today."
TIM FARGO

Time is of the essence because each day keeps coming and going no matter how you spend it. Time does not care if your day was well spent or if you have been swirling in negativity or inactivity.

> ### *Happiness and success are EARNED!*

People are not happy and successful by accident. It may be surprising how many defeating and destructive thoughts there are floating around in your head from the moment you wake up and guiding your path each day. However, on the days you wake up happy, it is good to pay attention to that feeling and remember that you build your happiness by continually investing in yourself.

> ### *You are that person in your dreams. You just need to start advancing those dreams to actualize them.*

You are accountable for yourself, but you also impact and influence those around you through your energy, words, and actions. If you think you don't have enough time for this effort, then you should consider this a requirement to help those you love. You can influence them by what you become, through investing in yourself and living out your purpose. It is so important for your loved ones to see that success can be realized, so they will be motivated and put the effort into realizing their own dreams.

> ### *Life is a continual process that unfolds over time.*

Life is a journey, so take time to savor your moments and be flexible as new experiences come into your life and your path shifts. Undoubtedly, events or people in your life will throw you off track here and there. Things will happen that are out of your control, but you must not allow people or events to sabotage you or hold you down. You must fight to stay on purpose for your ultimate best self by surrounding yourself with people who help build your confidence and support you.

You may be going through a tough time right now, feeling broken or thinking that you do not have the strength or tools to persevere. While you are the only one who knows what is in front of you at the moment, you are not alone. There is always someone you can help, someone who can help you, or someone who needs a friend. It is only a matter of time if you get yourself out in the community. If you feel alone, begin your journey by sharing yourself with others, and the world will start to guide you and provide the necessary tools for your success.

Let's open up our minds and commit to taking this journey together. You are meant for significance. If you fall or fail, do not surrender, as the valleys you experience are meant for growth in your life. Do not let others determine your value or ability to succeed. Show the world, and be your own superhero!

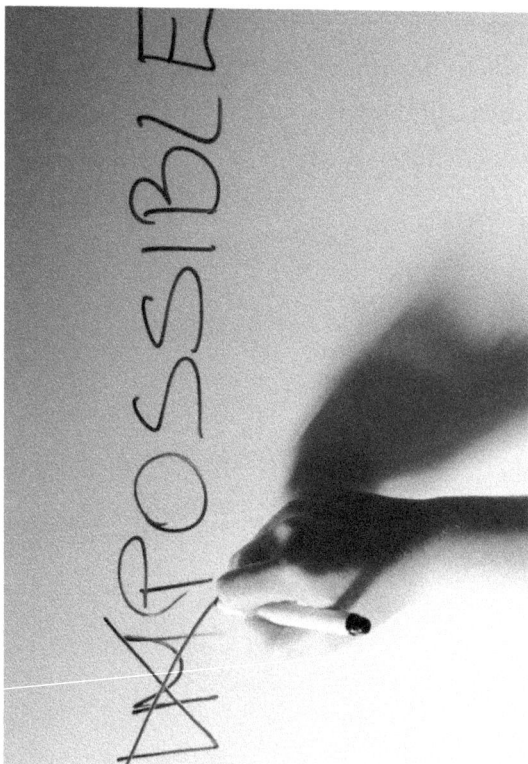

CHAPTER 3:

CLEARING THE COBWEBS: AN INDIVIDUAL ACTIVITY

*"If you don't design your own life plan,
chances are you'll fall into someone else's plan.
And guess what they have planned for you?
Not much."*

JIM ROHN

I want to share a simple activity with you. If done regularly, you can control your destiny and take charge of it. To gain from this activity, it is important for you to open your heart and mind to all possibilities. This will give you the opportunity to work toward an inspired future that you cannot easily contemplate today.

> ***Envision your true self without limits and expectations. You only have possibility on the inside!***

This fun activity will help you start each day by clearing out the cobwebs of any negative thinking that may be holding you back or bringing you down. It will also keep you focused on WHAT is important and WHY it is important. By working through this inspiring activity, you can start every day focused on your purpose and with a plan to achieve your most ambitious dreams!

I recommend you do this activity as often as possible to stay in touch with yourself and keep on track for achieving inspired action. Best of all, it only takes a few minutes and can be done while drinking your coffee or can easily be included in your morning routine.

Let's get started:

Below are instructions for an individual activity with a visual example. The instructions are not meant to be exhaustive, but should be utilized as a starting guide. Please remember to have fun and make this your own!

Now

- Too many bills
- Health challenges
- Don't want to go to work
- Too busy
- Need to work out
- Need a date or date night
- Need to win the lottery
- In-laws - ughhhhh

?.?

Future

- Beach
- New House (further away from in-laws)
- Meditation & Yoga Daily
- Girls/Guys Night
- Vacation in Maui
- Inspiring job
- Extra spending money $
- Maid :)

Gratitude:

1.) Shelter, job, family & friends
2.) Gym close by
3.) Ability to advance my education

Quote:

"When writing your story of life, don't let anyone else hold the pen."
    - Zig Ziglar

Affirmations:

1.) I am so happy to be in Maui having fun in the sun.
2.) I am so thankful to be moving into my new dream home by the beach.

Actions:

1.) Start researching new houses and towns
2.) Schedule girls/guys night
3.) Renew budget to look for ways to save or make room for a maid, so I can use that time to go back to school.

Celebrate:

I am working towards a new, inspired future!

Individual Activity:

1. On the ***left portion*** of the whiteboard, draw ***two columns*** (see previous visual example).

   - Title the ***first column*** as <u>NOW</u> and write down all the thoughts floating around in your head. You can also draw pictures. This is meant to clear your mind.

     o <u>Optional warm-up activity</u>: Take a few minutes to imagine your ultimate day and describe what you would experience if everything you can imagine for yourself was a reality, without any limits, and all of your dreams were realized.

       Write the thoughts on the ***far-right portion*** of the whiteboard (see example where it says gratitude) or on a separate piece of paper. If using the whiteboard, after you complete the FUTURE column, take a picture of this optional activity for later reference and then erase it to create space to complete the individual activity.

- Title the **_second column_** on the left portion of the board as <u>FUTURE</u> and start brainstorming about what it would be like and what would be in your mind if you were living your dreams and experiencing the ultimate life you can imagine for yourself (refer to optional activity above).
  - ○ Write down everything that comes to mind. Be genuine to

your nature, but not too limiting.

o Our future identity will be built on a new path, so don't focus only on the current view. This activity is meant to challenge your imagination, so have fun with it.

- After you finalize the FUTURE column, I suggest you employ a "clearing method" on the NOW column in order to maintain focus on the future you are designing for yourself. It may take you several days of working through this activity before some undesired items fall further down and eventually off of your list.

- On the NOW column, you can either erase the words completely or cross them out.

- If you erase, as you are physically erasing the whiteboard, picture yourself erasing any negative words from your mind and *most importantly your life.*

- If you cross out, you may want to only cross out the negative words. As you do this, visualize negative words and thoughts exiting your mind and *your life.*

- There are multiple techniques to use when clearing negativity from your life, but forgiveness and acceptance are the powerful methods I like to use.

  - Forgiveness of yourself and/or others.

    - This is a gift, as you are the only one paying a price for internalizing your poisons.

○ Accepting yourself, others, and/
or your reality.

  ▪ You can accept and move on
    towards inspired action, tak-
    ing lessons learned with you.

  ▪ Sometimes you must just ac-
    cept your realities and work
    your way around them so
    that they do not deny your
    inspired future.

○ You can write a letter of forgiveness and/or acceptance to get
the words out of your head and
move forward towards inspired
action.

  ▪ This letter can be sent, shred-
    ded, set on fire, or otherwise
    handled to eliminate it from
    your reality.

2. On the blank ***right portion*** of the whiteboard (see previous visual example), it's
   time to write down and develop the cat-
   egories to help you maintain focus and
   achieve the ultimate state described in
   the FUTURE column.

   Reminder: If you wrote on this portion
   of the whiteboard for the previous optional activity, please take a picture and
   then erase the information from the optional activity to have room for this portion of the individual activity.

   • Gratitude: List at least three words
     that express thoughts of gratitude in
     your life. If you find it challenging,
     make a list of areas people envy in
     your life to help you identify areas
     for gratitude.

   • Quote: Write an inspirational quote
     or religious/spiritual verse that

speaks to you. You can also do a finger pointing exercise. Ask for guidance, and then open any page of an inspirational book or scripture. Point with your finger to see the inspired message. It is also easy to search for quotes on the internet.

- Affirmation(s): Write down at least one affirmation to help make the future you envision a reality.
  - o For example, "I am so happy and grateful for making it onto a bestseller list."
  - o If you are not familiar with affirmations, I recommend that you look up examples on the internet.
  - o You will want to visualize as you speak the affirmation(s) all throughout your day.

- <u>Action(s)</u>: Write down at least one action you can take to advance your FUTURE column to becoming a reality.

- <u>Celebrate</u>: Write down at least one thing that you can celebrate about yourself. Today, this could be as simple as reading this material to advance yourself. DO NOT SKIP THIS STEP!

<u>Optional</u>: Personalize this activity, and feel free to add pictures or any other techniques that you find helpful because this is meant to be unique to you. You may also consider the following:

- Take a picture of your whiteboard and use it as a reminder of where you want to focus your efforts and thoughts. This allows you to look back over time to see your progress.

- If you are an auditory learner, record yourself reading this information.
- You can also record a selfie video acting "as if" you have already achieved your goals.
  - o For instance, if you want to buy a boat, rent one for a selfie video and talk about the new boat you just bought. Focus on the details for your video, like the clothing you will wear and the feelings you will experience while sailing.

If you consistently complete this individual activity, you will be amazed at what you can accomplish and how living with purpose can change your world. By changing your energy, you can even change how you see yourself and how others see you. Remember, your energy and that of those around you is infectious. Throughout your day, continually redirect from any negative or uninspired thinking by focusing on the whiteboard information from your individual activity.

COURAGE

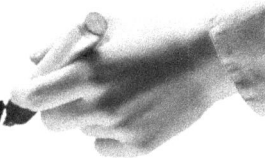

"You don't have to be great to start, but you have to start to be great."

Joe Sabah

CHAPTER 4:

WHITEBOARDS AND WHATEVER SHINDY

(Shindy - a lively party, large in spirit and opportunity)

"Nothing changes if nothing changes."
ERNIE LARSON

Self-discovery is so much fun! It can change the trajectory of your life, but only if you take the time to commit and engage. It is important to know yourself, but it is just as critical to know how you are perceived, both the good and the not so good.

> ### *Perception is just as important as reality.*

Perception shapes our experiences with people and the opportunities that are presented to us. This is why it is important to do group whiteboard activities with trusted people who are interested in your success in addition to the individual activities. So, let's plan a shindy!

> ### *Planning Your Whiteboards and Whatever Shindy*

"Great minds discuss ideas; average minds discuss events; small minds discuss people."
ELEANOR ROOSEVELT

It is important to get your foundation right before creating any plans.

What you need for the activities:

- Whiteboards and Whatever Group Organizer, Shindy Host(ess) and Shindy Captain (consider hiring a life coach)
- Location and refreshments
- Whiteboards (alternatively poster boards or paper), dry-erase markers, paper and pen, and optional portable easel (BYOW- Bring Your Own Whiteboard)

Whiteboards and Whatever Organizer responsibilities:

It is important to have a key organizer who is responsible for establishing the Whiteboards and Whatever core group by pulling the right people together and creating the framework for group connections and communications, as this can be very personal and emotional.

The organizer may consider having a membership, setting ground rules for trust and alignment, and requiring a confidentiality agreement.

These activities require openness, which means that trust is critical. Valuable and constructive input given in a sensible manner is important. A confidentiality agreement does not have to be a big deal. For convenience, a confidentiality agreement example can be downloaded at https://kimberlykelsoe.com. If done effectively, these activities can make a true impact.

Host(ess) and Captain responsibilities:

The Host(ess) is responsible for event planning and hosting a shindy, including setting topics and themes. The host(ess) must also create an environment to motivate, inspire, and entertain. It is best to either have a rotation for each shindy among the Whiteboards and Whatever group members or a sign-up sheet for each event.

The Captain (consider hiring a life coach) is responsible for keeping participants on track with the activities, inspiring participation, asking questions, leading activities, and stimulating creative thought for complex problem-solving.

Whiteboards and Whatever Shindy: Group Activities

A shindy can include fun and entertaining group activities described below to create a new vision for your future, based upon a creative approach to self-exploration and tools to ensure long-term success. There are many different types of groups who could benefit from the fun activities in a limitless number of topic areas, including:

- Professional, career, leadership, or influence
- Personal (i.e., bucket list or legacy) or spiritual

As you develop the list of trusted people for the group activities, keep in mind that those closest to you have great input. However, they also have their own opinions of you and may be driven by their own needs.

In the following, I lay out a suggested framework to develop out the shindy participants' vision for their life and a roadmap to make the vision a reality. While the following instructions are laid out for a group setting, you may also find it valuable to alter them to work through the activities individually.

See page 50 for an example of the outcome from this framework.

Let's get started:

Activity One: Brainstorm Key Words

The below instructions are meant to be led by the Captain for the participants.

1. To begin, the Captain should have the participants individually brainstorm about themselves and write their thoughts on their individual whiteboard. For instance, write their own gifts, talents, strengths, challenges, fears, desires, roadblocks, dreams, worries, and so on.

   - The Captain should have the participants take a few seconds to ask themselves "why" they wrote down what is there and if there is anything underlying that is a better fit.

   - Additionally, the Captain should ask participants to walk around to see if there is anything to contribute to others' brainstorming efforts. It is important to get others' input, with regards to who they are and what they have to offer, whether real or perceived.

- o <u>Hint for participants</u>: If you had to write one word or phrase in a fortune cookie about that person, what would it be? Is that information represented?

- o <u>Tip</u>: Participants should differentiate their feedback from the whiteboard owner by using a different colored marker.

2. Next, the Captain should have the participants walk around and identify one special word or phrase that best describes the whiteboard owner by circling it. The whiteboard owner can also circle up to three of their own words or phrases.

- If it is a smaller group, each participant should choose more than one item so that there are at least eight special words or phrases per whiteboard owner.

- After participants finish this part of the activity, the Captain should have each participant determine their own special word or phrase that uniquely stands out for them and place a star next to it. *This is their own guiding star from which other things will flow.*

  o <u>Tip for participant</u>: If this is a hard activity, they can consider what they would likely see on their tombstone.

The Captain should stop here and allow time for the participants to absorb and discuss the results of this activity. Then, participants can filter the information and open their imagination up to the key words or phrases in preparation for the next activity.

Activity Two: Analyze Inputs

After Activity One, everyone should be in alignment with their true self and how they are perceived. Participants' creative juices should be flowing at this point, so let's continue to build a plan. The Captain should instruct the participants to take a picture of their whiteboard and then erase it—except for the circled words/phrases and their guiding star.

Participants should take time to analyze the information for themselves. Below are some suggested questions the Captain should ask the participants to consider:

- Is there a pattern?
- Do you agree with what others contributed?

- Is there something missing? If so, what and why?
  - o You should consider adding it.
- What does this information tell you about yourself?
- How does your guiding star compare to those special words and phrases selected by others?

<u>Tip for participants</u>: I recommend participants write down notes, as they continue to brainstorm (i.e., roadblocks to be addressed).

This can be the end of the first shindy, or it could just be a coffee, wine, or snack break.

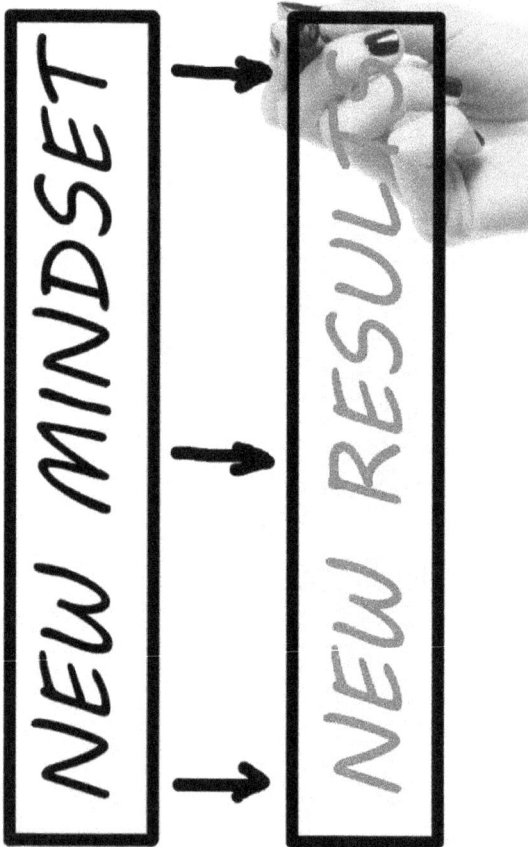

<u>Activity Three: Develop a Vision and Goals</u>

I would say this is where the real fun begins, but it's all fun when you actively work to create more joy in life. It is important to clarify the next steps by defining or refining the future participants envision, as well as the associated goals and objectives.

1. Below are some additional brainstorming questions the Captain should ask participants to consider for further brainstorming and taking notes for later reference:

   - What new opportunities, resources, and skills have you identified?

   - How can you use the results of the self-exploration activity to maximize your experiences and advance towards success?

   - What did you learn about yourself, and where will you want to take action in your life to accomplish your dreams?

- Where should you maintain focus in your life? What should you prioritize? What and where should you invest in yourself?

- What should be the new or refined vision for your future?

- What decisions should you make, or actions should you take?

- Is there something or someone standing in your way and blocking your path? How will you handle this situation?

- How do you take action to make your dreams come true? What resources are available to support your efforts?

- What are your next steps based on what the activity revealed?

At the end of this reflection, the Captain should ask the participants to erase the whiteboard, but take a picture for later reference. Participants may want to leave the guiding star written in a corner of the whiteboard throughout all activities.

2. On the top of the blank whiteboard, participants should be instructed to write one statement that illustrates the future vision for themselves.

   - The Captain should request each participant examine the vision statement to see how this relates to the brainstorming activities, if at all.

   - This may be at a macro or micro level, depending on what is desired to be achieved.

3. Under the vision statement, the Captain should have participants list three or four

goals (or achievements) to support the vision.

- It is important to set a timeline for goals and make them measurable, realistic, and achievable.

This is an individual activity, but if working with partners or a small group, this can be a great time to get feedback. The activity allows for refinement in preparation for Activity Four.

It may be a good time to stop here to go back and complete the individual activity in Chapter 3 to clear out negative words and thoughts before building the action plan below. It may also be good to absorb the information overnight before continuing to Activity Four.

Activity Four: Build an Action Plan

Now, it is time to build a plan with the information available. Shindy participants should be instructed to do the following:

1. Take a picture of the whiteboard with the vision and all the goals listed, then erase everything except the vision and the goal you plan to dive into first. This activity will be completed one goal at a time.

2. For each individual goal, the Captain should ask participants to write responses to the following on the whiteboard:

   - WHAT: This is your goal.
   - WHO: Who can help you achieve your goal, and what resources are available to you in your network?
   - WHEN: What is your timeline to make each goal happen?
   - WHERE, as relevant: Where will this take place, and/or where will

you be at the completion of achieving the goal?

- WHY: Why is this important to you and what do you expect to ultimately receive from focusing on it?
- HOW: There are different schools of thought here, including:
  - o Engage in positive thinking, faith, or ask for the HOW to be revealed to you, as your HOW may not be fully apparent to you yet.
  - o You can make plans on the HOW, but you know life will happen. So, you need to make your plans flexible.
  - o You are in control of your destiny. Your choices for action are critical. *The most important part*

of the HOW is getting started and taking action today.

o Be creative and keep adjusting the HOW to what your life brings you. Keep your eyes open for signs of confirmation and follow your gut.

Participants will continue to dive deeper into each goal, as laid out above, one by one. As the goals are analyzed and the whiteboard filled up, the Captain will instruct participants to take a picture for later reference. Then, the Captain should have all participants erase everything, except for the vision and the first goal to build out. The participants may leave all of the goals on the whiteboard, if space allows (see final visual example below).

Vision - I will be a renowned artist selling paintings in the millions while enjoying life's little pleasures with my family

Goal 1: Complete art school, including Masters
Within
7 years
- Research and apply to the best art programs within 6 months
- Research scholarships within 3 months
- Find a mentor exhibiting the artistic success I strive to attain within one year

Goal 2: Mentor up-and-coming artists
starting
next year
- Connect with art programs and teachers within 6 months

Goal 3: Stress less about the little things to enjoy the now
- Yoga: go at least three times a month starting next month
- Meditation: at least 4 times a week starting next week for a minimum of 5 minutes - work up to 10 minutes within 6 months

3. The Captain should instruct each participant to do the following:
    - Write down each individual goal.
    - Under each individual goal, write down two to four steps to achieve your goal.
      - These should be detailed enough that you know exactly what you need to do and when.
      - This is a good time to gather others' input to make sure the goals are really reflective of the true vision you are trying to accomplish.
      - If space is tight, you can take a picture and erase the board to continue the activity for each goal individually.
    - At the end of the shindy, it is important for participants to be instructed

to write down the following in one place (see previous visual example):

- o Refined vision (your view of your future and what success looks like to you).
- o Goals to accomplish your vision (your what).
- o Steps you need to take to accomplish your goals.
- This activity completes the participants' roadmap to success!
  - o The Captain should ask if participants are spending energy on anything that does not follow their roadmap to success. If so, the Captain should ask them what they need to change in how they spend their time and/or with whom.

- Finally, it is recommended that participants turn the goals and objectives into affirmation(s) to repeat and visualize throughout the day to support inspired action and redirect from any negative thoughts.

Use what you have learned through these activities and you will accomplish more than you can imagine, as this effort turns into more dreams coming true for you.

MOTIVATION

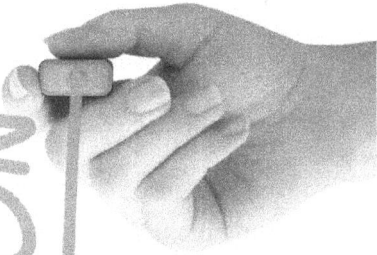

"*Excuses will always be there for you. Opportunity won't.*"

Anonymous

CHAPTER 5:

FINDING YOUR GEMS: A FINAL ACTIVITY

"If you obey all the rules, you miss all the fun."
KATHARINE HEPBURN

I am excited that you have reached this point in the book. You are now on your mission. You are running the race towards your goals, and no one can get in your way.

At this point, you likely have or are on your way to having a well-thought-out plan, but a plan is not of any value without accountability. You definitely want to be accountable to your plan, but the plan will shift over time because you change as you take action. New experiences will reveal new opportunities for you. As part of the Shindy and individually, accountability is key!

Activity Five: Ensure Accountability

In this last activity, let's focus on how you and your fellow shindy participants can enhance accountability, both individually and among the group. Some fun ideas for this include:

- Go to the whiteboards! Write down all of your brainstorming ideas on how you will make each other and yourself accountable.

- Give awards for the greatest progress or upon completion.

- Develop a buddy system. Remember, peer pressure works well!

CHAPTER 6:

TIME TO ENJOY YOUR SUCCESS

"If you can't fly then run, if you can't run then walk, if you can't walk then crawl, but whatever you do, you have to keep moving forward."
DR. MARTIN LUTHER KING, JR.

Remember to have fun, self-explore, grow, build your network, and ACHIEVE! No one should take these activities so seriously that they no longer have a stimulating environment for inspiring greatness and creativity.

Types of shindies to consider:

- "Whiteboards Shindy"
- "Whiteboards and Whatever Shindy"
- "Whiteboards and Wine Shindy"
- "Women and Whiteboards"
- "Whiteboards with Friends"
- "Whiteboards and Vision Boards"

Please make these activities your own, and then tell me all about it by emailing me at info@kimberlykelsoe.com. I will include many tips you provide via email or social media, by sharing them on my website at https://kimberlykelsoe.com to further inspire others' journey of empowerment.

Thank you, and I look forward to hearing from you on your successes and self-discovery journey. You can ACHIEVE and are WORTHY of so much more to SHARE with the world. Come join me today at https://kimberlykelsoe.com for more activities, my blogs, and more. I am ready to go on this journey with you to secure your dreams, starting now!

If you derived value from this material, please consider donating to Westonwood Ranch. For information, please see the back cover of this book. Please also include a note referencing this book on your donation.

ABOUT KIMBERLY

Kimberly Kelsoe has held numerous jobs since her teenage years, and for over fifteen years, she has successfully managed both mid-size and small teams in the corporate world. She is a sought-after mentor who relishes teaching and advancing others. Kimberly is also a daughter, wife, sister, and mother of teenage twin girls (Abigayle who has multiple disabilities and Natalie) who keep her quite busy.

Learning is her hobby, and she has earned multiple college degrees, including an MBA, JD, and LLM. Kimberly has taken calculated risks that have proven successful on her path from hostess and waitress to attorney. She has also enjoyed taking on multiple new positions outside of her area of expertise for growth opportunities, even after landing a dream job. She is living proof that you can have more than one sweet spot in your life and career.

Growing up, Kimberly lived in a number of states in which she re-created her identity over and over. This taught her many lessons. She moved from the East Coast to the West Coast and back recently, which has been very rewarding for her and her family in so many ways. Currently she is in a field government affairs role, which requires lots of juggling between family, work, her own needs, and a crazy travel schedule.

Kimberly is not your typical author, mentor, or coach. You can consider her to be like a guardian angel, slightly nudging you in one direction or another until you find your own path of bliss and boundless energy. You will feel like you are in a friendly conversation, simple thought, or sharing your life stories, but you will be discovering your inner desires and passions previously buried deep inside you. She is very passionate about helping people discover their full potential and celebrating it through taking action.

Through Kimberly's experiences, she discovered many life lessons, tips, and perspectives that she enjoys sharing with her loved ones and is now sharing through her written words. Becoming a published author is fulfilling a long-held dream and passion for Kimberly, and it advances her goals in other areas that are inspired by her daughters.

* 9 7 8 1 9 4 6 6 2 9 5 9 3 *